DO YOU BELIEVE?

D1366647

DO YOU BELIEVE?

THE CHALLENGE OF AN EASTER FAITH

ANDREW NUGENT, OSB
FOREWORD BY Joan Chittister, OSB

Paulist Press
New York / Mahwah, NJ

Cover image: Easter Lily flowers, © David Carillet / Shutterstock.com
Cover design by Trudi Gershenov
Book design by Lynn Else

Library of Congress Cataloging–in–Publication Data

Nugent, Andrew.
    Do you believe? : the challenge of an Easter faith / Andrew Nugent, OSB ; foreword by Joan Chittister.
        pages cm
    ISBN 978-0-8091-4907-0 (pbk. : alk. paper) — ISBN 978-1-58768-450-0 (ebook)
    1. Holy Week—Meditations. 2. Benedict, Saint, Abbot of Monte Cassino. I. Title.
    BT414.N84 2014
    242`.35—dc23

                                                                    2014018724

ISBN 978–0–8091–4907–0 (paperback)
ISBN 978–1–58768–450–0 (e–book)

Published by Paulist Press
997 MacArthur Boulevard
Mahwah, New Jersey 07430

www.paulistpress.com

Printed and bound in the
United States of America

To the monks of St. Benedict's Monastery,
Ewu–Ishan, Nigeria.
*"Wherever we may be, we are united in the service
Of the same Lord"* (RB 61:10).

CONTENTS

FOREWORD
DO YOU BELIEVE?
AND IF SO, HOW AND WHAT?

Somewhere in the course of the spiritual life every Christian has to make a decision about Lent.

The problem is that there are more ways than one to think about Lent; more ways than one to describe the way it must be celebrated. Lent, like everything else in life, has evolved over time. Each of its many expressions along the way reflects the culture and times of the period. Each of them—from the period of the Passion Plays to today's Palm Sunday processions—is serious and spirit-filled. But different.

At the end of the day, then, whatever the style of Lent is in practice at various times or in various places around the world, the way we live Lent will have something to do with the way we see holiness, the way we see Jesus, and the way we see life.

In our time, in this era between the end of Vatican I and the developments of Vatican II, we have two basic options—one in which we were raised, and one that is emerging: We can go through life looking at Lent as that long, grim, penitential season that casts a low, dim shadow over life. Or we can understand Lent as a time of new discipleship, a new way of understanding holiness, a new way of seeing Easter.

We can come to realize that all of life is holy and that Lent is simply a renewed awareness of that life. Or, we can go on seeing the Lenten season as a kind of life-denying project that puts a damper on life as well as good times.

The fact is that this dark, stringent definition of Lent comes heavily colored by the experiences of the Desert Monastics of the third to fifth centuries. The movement to the deserts of Egypt was not a mark of early Christianity. It came as a response to the legalization of Christianity by the Emperor Constantine.

After almost three hundred years of oppression, persecution, and rejection, Christianity could finally come out of the shadows. It was legal now to be a Christian. In fact, the Emperor himself converted to Christianity. That move shook the Western world. It not only made Christianity legal but, for many reasons, fashionable, touted, and popular, as well.

Christians, who had suffered persecution, or faced martyrdom and had to live sequestered from the public arena, were suddenly disturbingly mainstream. In the midst of a fast-growing Christian population far removed from the simple, communal life they had known in early Christian communities, they found themselves spiritually marooned.

As a result, Christians long accustomed to being "different," and distinct from the populations around them, saw what they considered to be the corruption of the Christian ideal. Now what was left of it, they considered to be, at best, a mediocre imitation of the real thing.

What became known as the "flight to the desert" began.

The question now became how to live an intensely Christian life in a world without martyrdom; a world where being Christian was no longer a matter of life or death.

For some Christians, the answer was simply to leave the cities entirely. They withdrew to the desert to live the Christian life, totally removed from what they saw as the sinful, conventional, sometimes pedestrian society around them.

At that moment, the struggle between the desert and the city began in the Christian mind. The question of whether or not it was even possible to be a serious Christian in the city, in the midst of wealth and distraction, frivolity and feasting, became central.

The answer of the Desert Monastics to that question was a clear one. In their minds at that time in history, the Christian life, the pursuit of union with God, demanded separation from the world, asceticism—a life of self-denial, and contemplation or total immersion in the Word of God. Asceticism became the bridge between the era of the martyrs and the time of Christian ascendancy.

Eventually, Lent became the carrier of that spirituality to the church at large. So began the concentration on "self-denial," and "separation from the world"—which meant, chiefly, "fasting" and "abstinence," and giving up activities that were enjoyable. Movies, candy, and celebrations were replaced with prayers.

However, some groups, the Benedictines in particular, took a completely different approach to Lent, as Father Andrew so well explains in Chapter Nine, "A Benedictine Easter."

Benedict's Rule for lay Benedictine communities in the fifth and sixth centuries did not focus Lent on suffering and sheer self-denial. Benedict focused Lent on Easter, on preparation for the fullness of life—both here and hereafter.

The Benedictine Rule called for more consciousness of what daily life demands, and more commitment to the regular elements of the Christian life. Most of all, the Rule requires serious, knowledgeable, and personal immersion in the Gospels and reflection on the relationship of these Holy Week scriptures to our own daily lives.

Like the Christians of those early centuries, *Do You Believe?*, this small guide of Father Andrew's, takes us through the scriptures of Holy Week. It helps us find ourselves in them. No, Lent and Holy Week are not about playing let's-pretend-we're-in-first-century-Jerusalem. We are being much more serious than that. We are called here and now to apply to our own lives what happened there.

Then, when Easter Sunday finally arrives we will all be more prepared to go on living when it's over. We will see life as good, not to be rejected. We will see Jesus as the one who calls us to fullness of life, not its denial. We will see holiness as the ability to live deeply and consciously the life of Jesus in our own times.

Happy Easter! Indeed, Alleluia is our cry.

Joan Chittister, OSB

INTRODUCTION

This is a book about Easter. My publishers were keen that the title be in the interrogative. I cannot remember whether that is a *voice* or a *mood*—perhaps it is both. None of us was doubtful or tentative about the Easter Mystery itself, but we were conscious that this is "Holy Ground" where we should at least "remove our sandals" (Exod 3:5).

St. Augustine rejoices that "we are an Easter People and Alleluia is our Song." We must nevertheless always be conscious that we possess this treasure in earthenware jars, to be shared—and never, as a trophy, to be brandished. Great is the mystery of our faith! An elderly monk of our own congregation says in wonder each year when the whole Paschal celebration has run its course: "And to think that I thought that I understood Easter!"

"So who am I?" asked Pope Francis in another context, where a bit of humility was also appropriate. I want to offer two other introductory explanations.

First, why begin a book about Easter with a chapter about the transfiguration? This is because the transfiguration of Jesus is surely a prophetic anticipation of the glory of the resurrection. It is clear from the gospel record that the disciples of Jesus were increasingly bewildered, and eventually dumb-founded, as the events of Holy Week unfolded. They seem to have spent most of their time running away from those events, psychologically, spiritually, and soon literally. Their disarray was almost complete. We can say that they *needed* the transfigura-tion, this anticipated glorification of their Lord. And so also do we at various times in our lives. I think this explains the prominent position in the Gospels of the transfiguration, and why it is important to include it in any meditation on Easter.

Second, why the long chapter on St. Benedict's Easter? Well, that is where I am coming from myself as a Benedic-tine monk. The advice given to every budding author is "write about what you know." But let me quote somebody more authoritative than myself, Abbot Denis Huerre, who was abbot of La Pierre-qui-Vire Monastery in France for twenty years before becoming president of the Benedictine Congregation of Subiaco. Abbot Denis writes:

> The genius, and so the greatness, of Benedict lies in the way he was able to center the whole of monastic life, even as an organized structure, on the single mystery of Easter and Pentecost, on what is revealed by this vista unblocked and opened by Christ and the Holy Spirit.[1]

What is true of monastic life is true even more of Christian life, which is centered on and in that same Paschal Mystery.

---

1. Denis Huerre, *Letters to my Brothers and Sisters* (Collegeville, MN: The Liturgical Press, 1994), 40.

CHAPTER 1

THE TRANSFIGURATION

*"This is my Son, the Beloved; with him I am well pleased;
listen to him!"* (Matt 17:5b)

Each one of the Synoptic Gospels gives an account of the
transfiguration of our Lord, Jesus Christ (Matt 17:1–8; Mark
9:2–8; Luke 9:28–36). St. Peter's second letter insists on the
significance and the reliability of these accounts.

> For we did not follow cleverly devised myths when we
> made known to you the power and coming of our
> Lord Jesus Christ, but we had been eyewitnesses of his
> majesty. For he received honor and glory from God
> the Father when that voice was conveyed to him by
> the Majestic Glory, saying, "This is my Son, my
> Beloved, with whom I am well pleased." We ourselves
> heard this voice come from heaven, while we were
> with him on the holy mountain. (2 Pet 1:16–18)

The Fourth Gospel does not include an explicit account
of the transfiguration and glorification of Jesus, simply

1

because, as St. John himself explains in the Prologue to his Gospel, this is precisely what the entire Gospel is about.

> The Word became flesh
> and lived among us,
> and we have seen his glory,
> the glory as of a father's only son,
> full of grace and truth. (John 1:14)

We know that the Synoptic account of the transfiguration, which represents Moses and Elijah as present on the holy mountain with Jesus, is the evangelists' way of saying that the glorification of Jesus in the Easter event has been the summing up, the crescendo, the crowning of the whole of Salvation History, of the entire Law (Moses) and of the prophets (Elijah).

The transfiguration of Jesus is to be his glorification, and his great hour.

> The hour has come
> for the Son of Man to be glorified.
> Now my soul is troubled.
> And what should I say—
> "Father, save me from this hour"?
> No, it is for this reason that I have come to this hour.
> Father, glorify your name." (John 12:23, 27–28)

The Easter event—the passion, death, and resurrection of Christ—is indeed his glorification and his transfiguration.

FOR REFLECTION

1. "The Word became flesh and lived among us, and we have seen his glory." Have I had any perception of the "Word-became-flesh"? Have I seen his glory?
2. Has my compassion for and perception and understanding of people grown deeper in recent years?
3. Share or reflect on a transfiguration experience in your life.

CHAPTER 2
PALM SUNDAY

> *Let the same mind be in you that was in Christ Jesus,*
> *who, though he was in the form of God, did not regard*
> *equality with God as something to be exploited, but*
> *emptied himself, taking the form of a slave, being born*
> *in human likeness.* (Phil 2:5–7)

Palm Sunday is like Easter Sunday in reverse. Instead of *Per Crucem ad Lucem*, "through the cross to the resurrection," which is the crowning of our Easter joy, we celebrate on Palm Sunday, first, the triumphal entry of Jesus into Jerusalem and, only then, we read solemnly one of the Synoptic accounts of his betrayal, suffering, and death. What a reversal of precedence, if not of priorities! Yet, that is the way it did happen—from Sunday to Sunday—and it is commemorated in the same context: the celebration of the Eucharist, which means "thanksgiving."

Holy Week can have this same effect on us, if we let it. It can turn us upside down, even inside out. And perhaps this is the way it should be. That first Holy Week certainly sorted out the men from the boys among the most intimate friends and disciples of Jesus. In terms of betrayal, treachery, craven cowardice, and frantic running away, it is almost like a grim comedy. The supporters of Jesus, when they saw him, at last, apparently willing to confront the powers that be and to go public about his own claims were on a high. They were practically dancing in the street. They were singing at the top of their voices:

> Hosanna to the Son of David!
> > Blessed is the one who comes in the name of
> > the Lord!
> Hosanna in the highest heaven!   (Matt 21:9)

The Old City of Jerusalem was a very compact space. To speak of walls or gates before the sixth century AD would be quite an anachronism, but we can assume that to stage a triumphal entry through any of the main thoroughfares of the city would have provoked quite a stir. St. Matthew says in his account of the events: "When he entered Jerusalem, the whole city was in turmoil." We can believe it.

St. Luke records that the Pharisees in the crowd, obviously judging that what was happening was way over the top, said to Jesus, "Teacher, order your disciples to stop." They were shocked and warned him. But Jesus replied, "I tell you, if these [his disciples] were silent, the stones would shout out" (Luke 19:39–40).

Theologically or spiritually, this may have been an appropriate response to what was happening. But politically, Jesus, by allowing himself to play the central role in such a spectacle, seemed to be making some kind of a bid for power. He was clearly perceived to be throwing down a direct challenge to both the Jewish and the Roman authorities. Moreover he must have known that this was how his behavior would be interpreted both by the civil and religious powers—and indeed by the large majority of the crowd that had mustered around him.

If Jesus were not actually signing his own death warrant, he must have known that the time had come for the inevitable confrontation with powerful and hostile forces that he had been consciously avoiding during his ministry in Galilee, in Samaria, and even further afield.

All three Synoptic Gospels record the fact that Jesus told the twelve apostles specifically that he was going up to Jerusalem to die. Mark says that those who followed him were afraid (Mark 10:32). On the other hand, Luke claims that "they understood nothing about all these things; in fact, what he said was hidden from them, and they did not grasp what was said" (Luke 18:34).

Holy Week chronicles the political maneuvering among the Jewish authorities, with their "rent-a-mob" collection of roughnecks; the Roman occupying forces and Pontius Pilate, their Governor; King Herod, who was eager to meet Jesus and to check out whether he might be John the Baptist come back to life, after Herod had beheaded him; and Judas, the traitor, on the make—each with their different agendas and self-centered motives. Finally, thrust into all this miasma of conflicting interests and emotions were the disciples of Jesus, mostly simple men, who were to be overwhelmed by what was just about to hit them, and Jesus, himself.

Bethphage, Bethany, and the Mount of Olives are given as reference points in the various Gospel accounts and are all located to the east of Jerusalem; so also is the Garden of Gethsemane. It is assumed that Jesus would have approached the Old City down the Mount of Olives, coming from the east side, for his triumphal entry. He probably crossed into the city in the vicinity of the present Lions' Gate, where he would have found himself close to the Temple Mount and to what was to become known in later years as the *via dolorosa*, "the way of the cross," leading to Golgotha.

And so the paradox with which we started: the triumphal entry and death as an outcast is subsumed, through the very path that Jesus takes to Jerusalem, into a higher logic, or a deeper spirituality: the triumphal entry into the way of the cross, where Christ the King reigns from the wood of the cross.

Is this not what Holy Week and Easter are about—the triumph of the supreme sacrifice of love?

FOR REFLECTION

1. Did Jesus play his cards right on Palm Sunday?
2. Do you think that Jesus deliberately provoked the Roman and Jewish authorities?
3. St. Peter tried to advise Jesus to be more diplomatic (Matt 16:21–23). How would you have advised him?

CHAPTER 3
HOLY THURSDAY

As often as you eat this bread and drink the cup, you
proclaim the Lord's death until he comes. (1 Cor 11:26)

Apart from Jesus, only one other person appears in the
gospel reading every day in Holy Week until Good Friday.
That person is Judas Iscariot. We are witnessing the clash of
opposites, of good and evil, of love and selfishness.

Jesus is the one who trusts his Father, and obeys. On the
Wednesday of Holy Week, we see him accept anointing
with precious ointment for his burial. This means he knows
and accepts that he is going to die. We are told that the fra-
grance of that anointing fills the whole house. This says that
his acceptance is a sweet-smelling sacrifice to the Father, and
for our sakes (John 12:1–8).

Judas Iscariot does not agree. His pretended concern for
the poor—"Why was this perfume not sold for three hundred denarii and the money given to the poor?"—is pure
hypocrisy (John 12:5). He kept the common purse for the

9

little group of disciples, and regularly stole what was put into it. But, as often happens in life, Judas is hiding behind the righteous indignation, even anger, of other disciples who do not understand and also think that the precious ointment is being wasted (Matt 26:6–13; Mark 14:3–9).

However, Judas has more fundamental reasons for his rejection of what Jesus is doing. Judas is allergic to death, and to failure. He has no use for a leader who is going to die. The first of all the disciples, he now understands what is about to happen—that Jesus really is going to die, voluntarily; that he is going to accept failure. For Judas, the pragmatist, this is not acceptable. The only question remaining is how to salvage something out of this looming disaster. The fact is that Judas betrays Jesus because, in his view, Jesus has already betrayed himself.

Today, Holy Thursday, Jesus who is *Lord and Master*, kneels to wash the feet of his disciples. This is the menial service of a slave. It is the prelude to the total gift of himself, which Jesus will make in the Last Supper and on the cross when he gives his own flesh and blood for our spiritual nourishment, and when he lays down his life for our salvation. Judas is also there at that Last Supper. Jesus washes his feet and feeds him with the bread of the Eucharist. Judas is not grateful. In fact, he probably despises what Jesus has become.

However, Judas is not the only one who disapproves of what Jesus is doing.

> Jesus came to Simon Peter, who said to him, "Lord, are you going to wash my feet?" Jesus answered, "You do not know now what I am doing, but later you will

understand." Peter said to him, "You will never wash my feet." (John 13:6–8)

We admire Peter's humility, his reverence for Christ, his indignant, almost angry loyalty to him—or perhaps we should say his loyalty to the Christ whom *he* wants Jesus to be, but whom Jesus refuses to impersonate. In fact, as the time of Jesus' passion and death draws near, a major difference, a major disagreement between Jesus and even his closest disciples is coming out into the open. There is no sign here that Jesus is grateful for Peter's angry loyalty. He neither thanks him nor compliments him. On the contrary, Jesus confronts Peter with a stark choice: "Unless I wash you, you have no share with me." Faced with that ultimatum, Peter submits. The problem is solved, but only for the moment.

The incomprehension, the opposition even, of the disciples about who Jesus really is and what he actually intends to do has persisted and become focused over three years. After all that time, while the disciples have learned so much (Matt 11:25–27; Luke 10:21–24), their minds and hearts are still earthbound.

Most of the disciples still probably want a political Messiah who will drive out the Romans and make their dreams come true. They rejoice that the demons obey them, rather than that their names are written in heaven (Luke 10:20). They want to call down fire and brimstone on those who do not receive them, ignorant of the spirit to which they belong (Luke 9:54–55). Even on the road to Calvary, they are still arguing about which of them is the greatest (Mark 9:33–34), and even such worthy disciples as James and John push their poor mother to coax Jesus to nominate her two sons to the top positions in his kingdom. The other ten apostles are in no doubt about whose great idea that was (Matt 20:24; Mark 10:35–45). This must be the first recorded example of that clerical ambition, which has become such a time-honored tradition in the Church!

"Do you still not understand?" Christ cries out to his disciples so many times.

When Jesus begins to talk about his sufferings and death, these same disciples are horrified:

> From that time on, Jesus began to show his disciples that he must go to Jerusalem and undergo great suffering at the hands of the elders and chief priests and scribes, and be killed, and on the third day be raised. And Peter took him aside and began to rebuke him, saying, "God forbid it, Lord! This must never happen to you." (Matt 16:21–22)

This is the same concern that we are to see on Holy Thursday when Jesus kneels to wash the feet of his disciples. Peter's determination is to preserve his Master from this loss of face, this humiliation, this gift of himself.

What separates Peter's attitude from that of Judas? One is a traitor, the other is loyal—and that is no small difference—but both feel that Jesus is embarking on a way that is foolish and wrong. Note the harshness of Jesus' reply to Peter: "Get behind me, Satan! You are a stumbling block to me; for you are setting your mind not on divine things but on human things" (Matt 16:23). This must be the harshest rebuke that Jesus ever addresses to anyone in the Gospels.

Remember the words spoken by Simeon to Mary, when she came to present her child to God in the Temple:

> "This child is destined for the falling and the rising of many in Israel, and to be a sign that will be opposed so that the inner thoughts of many will be revealed—and a sword will pierce your own soul too." (Luke 2:34–35)

We are not mere spectators at these events of Holy Week. The sword will pierce our souls, too, and the secret thoughts of our hearts will be laid bare. On Holy Thursday and on Good Friday, we must learn to accept a Savior who is not powerful, but weak, and who kneels to wash our feet. That washing is more powerful than any work of power. We must accept to have a part (*meros*) with a Christ, who is not committed to our ideas of earthbound success or happiness. This is the implication of our baptism, of our commitment to a Christ who goes to his death, and who allows us to go to ours.

This acceptance brings us to the second part of the Holy Thursday mystery, the Eucharist, the gift of Christ's body and blood, of his whole life and death as *our* life and death, of his whole being as *our* being.

> "I am the living bread that came down from heaven. Whoever eats of this bread will live forever; and the bread that I will give for the life of the world is my flesh." (John 6:51)

Remember the reaction of many when Jesus first spoke of this great gift of God: "This teaching is difficult; who can accept it?" (John 6:60). And many of his followers walked away.

Jesus asks us, "Do you also wish to go away?" (John 6:67). This is our Holy Week choice. Do we want to turn our backs on a Christ who, ultimately, has nothing to offer except his flesh and blood, himself, and his priceless gifts of faith, hope, and love?

May we have the faith to reply with Peter, "Lord, to whom can we go? You have the words of eternal life. We have come to believe and know that you are the Holy One of God" (John 6:68–69).

FOR REFLECTION

1. As quoted from St. Paul at the opening of this chapter, how do "we proclaim the Lord's death" by being at Mass?
2. Did Jesus have a death wish?
3. What does the event of the washing of the feet mean?
4. What was Jesus so anxious for his disciples to understand when he asked, "Do you still not understand?"

CHAPTER 4
LIGHT AND DARKNESS

> *Jesus answered, "You say that I am a king. For this
> I was born, and for this I came into the world, to testify
> to the truth. Everyone who belongs to the truth listens to
> my voice." Pilate asked him, "What is truth?"*
> (John 18:37–38)

Those who sin against the light become darkness. Herod
and Pontius Pilate both sinned against the light that had
been given to them, and so both became darkness.

There is this direct connection between the way that
Herod treated the precursor of the Messiah, John the
Baptist, and the way that he was to treat the Messiah himself, Jesus Christ, the Son of God. Herod knew that John the
Baptist was a holy man. The Gospel tells us that he was puz-
zled by John, but that he liked to listen to him. In fact, here
was a real possibility that Herod might have grown into the
truth, if only he had acted in accordance with that little
truth of which he already had an intuition. But what happened?

Remember the dancing girl and her bloodthirsty mother? Herodias, the dancing girl's mother, hated John the Baptist because John had told Herod the truth, as he saw it, about Herod's illegitimate marriage to his brother's wife, who was Herodias herself. She was furious with him and wanted to kill him, but was unable to do so, because Herod knew that John was a righteous man, and he shielded him from her vengeful anger.

At last, Herodias got her chance—Herod's birthday party (Matt 14:3–12; Mark 6:17–29)! He gave a banquet for his courtiers and officers and for the leaders of Galilee. Everybody who was anybody was there. The girl came in and danced. "She pleased Herod and his guests." Herod, clearly under the very temporary impression that everybody loved him, which, historically, was far from the case, had also very probably been drinking far too much wine. He swore a ridiculous oath to the girl, promising to give her anything she asked, even half of his kingdom. Prompted by her mother, the girl requested, "I want you to give me at once the head of John the Baptist on a platter."

According to the Gospel account, Herod was "deeply grieved," but thinking of the reckless oath he had sworn, and of his guests, he decided to stifle the voice of conscience, and to murder that good and holy man. Herod sinned against the light, and at that precise moment, he became darkness.

When Jesus, in turn, began to be noticed, he came to Herod's attention as a matter of course. Herod was the tetrarch of Galilee, and carefully monitored the religious excitements in his territories because these were a potential and powerful source of friction between the Roman overlords and their Jewish subjects. Furthermore, Herod had not forgotten John the Baptist. When Jesus came preaching and working wonders only a few months later, Herod began to imagine that he must be John the Baptist, whom he had murdered at the behest of a dancing girl, or of her harridan of a mother, and who must have risen from the dead. Herod was anxious to see Jesus (Luke 9:9). He was even hoping that, if Jesus really were John, he would not resent too much the fact that he had already murdered him once, and might even unbend sufficiently to work an interesting miracle just for him (Luke 23:8). This is already an indication of how really blind he had become.

When Pilate sent Jesus to Herod after his arrest, Herod, we are told, was *delighted*. He questioned Jesus at length, but Jesus did not answer him one word in reply. So Herod and his guard treated Jesus with contempt, made fun of him, and sent him back to Pilate dressed like a fool. Who was the real fool?

St. Luke has an interesting footnote to this narrative: "That same day Herod and Pilate became friends with each other; before this they had been enemies" (Luke 23:12). The Irish have a proverb: *Aithníonn ciaróg ciaróg eile*, which means "One cockroach recognizes another." We could say in this context that one who lives in *darkness* recognizes another who lives the same way. At best, their newfound friendship could be compared to crooked honor among thieves.

The historical Pilate was not an attractive person. "The sources describe him as cruel, coldhearted, and rigid."[1] And yet, as in the case of Herod and the Baptist, Pilate, too, was offered a perception of the truth. All four Gospels agreed that Pilate was convinced that Jesus, like John, was an upright man, and possibly a prophet.

As governor, Pilate was judge and jury. He tried to evade his responsibility by passing Jesus over to Herod. When that expedient failed, and when he even seemed to have a riot on his hands, stirred up by the chief priests and their cronies, and above all, when Pilate heard the menacing cry from the Jews: "If you release this man, you are no friend of the emperor. Everyone who claims to be a king sets himself against the emperor," Pilate has heard enough! Like Herod in the case of John the Baptist, Pilate chose to sin against the light, and condemned Jesus to be crucified (John 19:1–16).

In a way, Pilate had foreshadowed his own blindness. In one of his interrogations, Jesus said, "Everyone who belongs to the truth listens to my voice." Pilate asked grotesquely, "What is truth?" (John 18:37–38). Jesus, who is the way, the truth, and the life, is standing inches in front of his nose—and Pilate cannot see him.

As for the newfound friendship between Pilate and Herod, we can only quote a saying that Jesus himself uses in a similar context: "Can a blind person guide a blind person? Will not both fall into a pit?" (Luke 6:39).

---

1. Reza Asan, *Zealot: The Life and Times of Jesus of Nazareth* (New York: Random House, 2013), 46.

FOR REFLECTION

1. Can people become blind or deaf spiritually?
2. Can you give examples of such blindness from history or from the Bible?
3. What steps can we take to avoid this happening to us or to those about whom we care?

CHAPTER 5

GOOD FRIDAY

> *Let us run with perseverance the race that is set before us,*
> *looking to Jesus the pioneer and perfecter of our faith, who*
> *for the sake of the joy that was set before him endured the*
> *cross, disregarding its shame.* (Heb 12:1–2)

What joy do we look forward to in the future? What do we hope for? The Church's essential mission is to give people hope. But in order to know true hope, we need a conversion of heart. Jesus said, "Where your treasure is, there your heart will be also" (Matt 6:21).

Where is our treasure? Where is the focus of our hope? Hope and faith are inseparably linked. Good Friday is the day of the year that sorts us out; that forces us to ask what we really believe in? What do we really hope for?

We know that at the beginning of Christ's passion, the Agony in the Garden, his chosen disciples sleep. We cannot believe that this is sheer callousness or indifference. St. Luke uses a curious phrase about this. He says that the disciples are "sleeping because of grief" (Luke 22:45). I think he is talking about what modern psychology calls denial. When we are faced with something so alien to what we believe in, so contrary to everything we hope for—a reality that threatens to blow our minds—we simply go into denial and switch off.

When the disciples see their Master, who has always been so strong and in control, now in the garden, so afraid, so defenseless, and so anguished that, as St. Luke tells us, "his sweat became like great drops of blood falling down on the ground," they just distance themselves from it; they cannot cope with it (Luke 22:39–46). It is too contrary, too different from what they want to see and experience, and too opposed to what they believe in and what they hope for.

As the drama of that night and the next day heightens, it is as if a great wedge is being driven between Christ and his disciples. He is plumbing the depths of what it means to be human; they back off in horror from him and from their own humanity. The mob arrives. Jesus is dragged away to his trial, to torture, and to death, while those who had vowed, to a man, that they were ready to die with him, take to their heels and abandon him. Peter even went to the extreme of denying three times that he had ever even known Jesus.

What are we dealing with here? Why did Jesus' disciples desert him? Why did Peter deny him? Is it because they were all cowards? Is that it? Interestingly, Jesus never accused his disciples of cowardice. Indeed, just a few hours later, he is to tell Pilate with perhaps even a touch of pride, "If my kingdom were of this world, my followers would be fighting to keep me from being handed over to the Jews" (John 18:36). And, to be fair to Peter, he not only said that he would fight to save

Jesus, he meant what he said, and he actually *did* it. He *did* fight—and against hopeless odds—professional soldiers of the Roman Legion. So what went wrong?

The real problem for Peter, for the disciples, and for each of us, is not about cowardice or courage. The problem is about hope and about faith. Jesus said to his disciples, "You will all become deserters because of me this night," or more literally, "You will be brought down, tripped up as by an obstacle" (Matt 26:31). It is not their courage that will fail them, but their faith. Jesus says it to Peter, "Simon, Simon, listen! Satan has demanded to sift all of you like wheat, but I have prayed for you that your own faith may not fail; and you, when once you have turned back, strengthen your brothers" (Luke 22:31–32).

Peter's problem, which is our problem too, is that he is only half converted. Peter has not "put on the mind of Christ." He clings obstinately to his own perspective. He wants a Christ who takes the easy way out; a Christ who cheats on what it means to be human. He wants a Christ who cannot be cornered, who cannot be the victim of human malice and cruelty. He wants a Christ–Superman who can never fail, never be overcome, and never die. In other words, he wants a Christ who is not human at all.

And when these hopes are shown to be illusory, Peter just cracks up. It is not just cowardice: it is the collapse of a whole world view.

The good news of the gospel is not that we are all going to be turned into Superman or Superwoman, but that God truly loves us and that we can trust him; that he is with us even in the very depths of our weakness, physical and moral. We can trust him in the face of all the evil that human wickedness can inflict upon us. We can trust him in sickness, in failure, and in death. We are not built to survive. We have to learn to let go, not in a spirit of quiet despair or stoical resignation, but in trust.

We have seen marvelous examples of this in our own family life: the faith of people in the face of great difficulties, and even death. That is human maturity in the richest sense. It is a slow conquest.

The serpent's temptation addressed to Eve was: "You will not die; for God knows that when you eat of it your eyes will be opened, and you will be like God, knowing good and evil" (Gen 3:4–5). In other words, God is a liar. Do not trust him. He does not love you enough. He has deprived you of something that would make you happier and more fulfilled. Do it your way! The essence of every sin is this belief that we can do better, go further and faster, on our own.

In a sense, Christ's death is an absurdity. Peter and Judas are right about that. Jesus is the victim of the nasty minded calculations of third-rate politicians. The fact that it is stupid— and Jesus himself stated as much: "Father, forgive them; for they do not know what they are doing" (Luke 23:34)—does not make it any less lethal. Humanly speaking, Jesus, like Eve, is tempted to think that God has got it wrong, and is doing him wrong: "My God, my God, why have you forsaken me?" (Matt 27:46).

Faith and trust triumph. The dying words of Jesus: "Father, into your hands I commend my spirit" (Luke 23:46) are the perfect antithesis of all sin.

> O King of the Friday
> Whose limbs were stretched on the Cross,
> O Lord who did suffer
> The bruises, the wounds, the loss,
> We stretch ourselves
> Beneath the shield of thy might,
> Some fruit from the tree of thy passion
> Fall on us this night![2]

FOR REFLECTION

1. Is it good to suffer?
2. Is suffering meritorious?
3. What makes suffering meaningful?

---

2. An ancient Irish prayer, author unknown.

CHAPTER 6
HOLY SATURDAY

We have been buried with Christ by baptism into death,
so that, just as Christ was raised from the dead by the glory
of the Father, so we too might walk in newness of life.
(Rom 6:4)

In the days of my monastic youth, on Holy Saturday, some
of us used to climb a mountain: Galtee Mór, which is a serious climb, or else Keeper Hill, if we were feeling fragile or
the weather was uncertain. I suppose we didn't quite realize
it at the time, but this was a good way to stand back for a
few hours from the mysteries we had been celebrating so
intensely during the last several days, and to let them "fer-
ment," or sink in.

I wonder whether this was similar to what St. Peter was
trying to do when the primordial Easter event was chrono-
logically over—but would remain with Peter and with the
other disciples until their dying day, and forever. It remains,
too, with us latter-day disciples, so that it will ever deepen

our wonder, our understanding, our love and appreciation of that stupendous Easter event. So what did Peter do?

He said, "I am going fishing." And six other disciples felt the need to say, "We will go with you" (John 21:3).

Even the liturgy, which is both celebration and reflection on the Word of God and of his mighty deeds, needs to catch its breath occasionally. In other words, it does not only happen in temples or churches, nor through the medium of carefully predigested theological conceptualizations. The Word needs space and time and different mediums or mediations. Church people need to realize this when they are tempted to say censoriously that people today—and especially young people—have sold their souls for a cocktail of making money, sex, and trivial pursuits. This is simply not true. They may not find the heroic efforts of a practically geriatric, all-male, supposedly celibate clergy, including myself, of course, particularly relevant to where they are now in their own lives. Is that the real problem?

Regardless of how we view the current state of faith, we can surely agree that Holy Saturday is one day in the year when almost nothing is happening in churches until the Easter Vigil in the evening. It is a good day to climb mountains or go fishing. It is a good day to catch up with all that we have been experiencing.

Donal Walsh of Tralee, Co. Kerry—everyone in Ireland will know who I am talking about—climbed many of God's mountains. He has written and said that this has been one of the most meaningful activities to give him an insight into the "hero's" journey that the Lord had chosen for him to accomplish.[3] Everybody who has heard of him will recognize that he has indeed shared in the Easter Mystery of Jesus and has climbed hills and mountains from Calvary to Tabor.

When Donal Walsh was age twelve, he fell victim to a virulent bone cancer, which necessitated radical surgery and very severe chemotherapy. He fought back with incredible courage and, against all the odds, survived for four years, maintaining, in so far as possible, a normal lifestyle, his passionate interest in sports, and his very good friends, whom he described as like brothers to him. After three years of remission, the cancer reasserted itself, necessitating the removal of half a lung and more hideous chemotherapy. Weeks before his death, when he was very sick, Donal published an article, and then appeared on television, appealing to young people not to commit suicide because life was such an incredible gift. He was going to die soon, he said. He wished he could live to be one hundred, rear children, and play on the Munster Rugby Team. But he had no choice. The whole country, young and old, rose to his message; he was so manifestly sincere, so courageous, so unassuming, and just such a lovely, smiling young man.

From what I can gather, Donal was conventional in his religious practice, but he had firsthand experience that what happens in churches is only part of the story. I think that this is very important, especially as we try to understand young people in our own day. I will come back to this topic in chapter nine, when I try to come to grips with the young

---

3. I place the word *hero* in quotation marks because of Donal's insistence that he was neither brave nor a hero.

St. Benedict, who spent his late teens living in a cave. We have plenty of spiritual teen cave dwellers in our own day.

Let us return to an incident that St. Luke records in his Gospel. What is curious about this incident is Luke's choice of language. He says, "Once when Jesus was praying *alone, with only the disciples near him…*" (Luke 9:18–20). What exactly does Luke mean? Is Jesus alone, or is he in the presence of his disciples? If he means both, then it is certainly not *shared* prayer. No one is saying the Our Father! If you want to share somebody's prayer, you need to know roughly where he or she is coming from.

Perhaps this is precisely what Jesus is trying to achieve, to not be *alone* anymore when he prays, but to really connect with these disciples and friends. So he asks them two questions. The first question is rhetorical, to set a context for the second question. "Who do the crowds say that I am?" The disciples have no problem answering that question. They reply, "John the Baptist; but others, Elijah; and still others, that one of the ancient prophets has arisen." This is purely factual material, probably common knowledge amongst anyone and everyone associated with Jesus, and none of his followers is being asked to say where he, as an individual, stands in respect of any of these answers.

But Jesus asks a second question: "And who do you say that I am?" This time nobody answers—except Peter, who gives an acceptable response, "The Messiah of God" (Luke 9:18–20).

What does Peter mean, and how will this answer stand up to the crisis that is looming? We already have the answer to that further question on Good Friday. Judas betrayed Jesus for hard cash, Peter denied three times that he ever so much as knew him, and—to a man—the disciples turned tail and ran. The only one who stood at the foot of the cross was John and, of course, those wonderful women. This, as we have seen, was not so much a question of courage and cowardice, but a question of faith.

The situation is that Jesus has not long to live. He has done his best, both in words and deeds, to tell his disciples who he is, who his Father is, and why he has come into the world. He seems to have failed, both with his disciples, and with anyone who mattered in the world of politics and influence. He knows, too, that his earthly mission of preaching and healing is now over. It will pass to his disciples, and ultimately to us—to you and to me; because—and it must be noted—the postresurrection Jesus never appears to the crowds, never speaks a further word to them, never works any miracles for them. Yes, it is over—and indeed over *to us*.

We are tempted to imagine what the prayer of Jesus, still *alone*, must have been like. Was he not right to be almost despairing? "My God, my God, why have you forsaken me?" (Mark 15:34).

Some people, when they realize that this is "just" a quotation from Psalm 21, express the comfortable view that it is not to be taken too literally, as if Jesus were just reciting vespers. When one considers the almost comical disarray of the chosen disciples, and, looking further into the future, the darker side of Church history, including, to give just one example from our own day, the wretched scandal of pedophile priests and the massive arrogance and deviousness with which these crimes have been covered up in too many places, the wonder is at God's astounding patience and at the tenacious faith, hope, and love of Jesus, in spite of everything.

And yet, St. John, the beloved disciple, under the guidance of the Holy Spirit, describes beautifully in his Gospel what must have been the prayer of Jesus for his Church: "I ask not only on behalf of these, but also on behalf of those who will believe in me through their word, that they may all be one. As you, Father, are in me and I am in you, may they also be in us, so that the world may believe that you have sent me" (John 17:20–21).

Let us return to St. Peter and his fishing trip, which I depicted as practically a recreational, or at least a recuperative, exercise appropriate to Holy Saturday, a largely nonliturgical day. Even Jesus is resting in the tomb. However, as we shall see, the fishing trip happened, not on Holy Saturday, but when Jesus had already risen from the dead. So it cannot have happened as early as Saturday.[4]

The darker possibility is that Peter and his six companions were still unaware of the resurrection and were engaged in what they must have regarded as a crestfallen return to the real world of fishermen. In the words of Cleopas, one of the two disciples on the road to Emmaus, "We had hoped that he was the one to redeem Israel" (Luke 24:13–24). So

---

4. It is generally agreed among exegetes that it is impossible to establish a rigorous chronology of the postresurrection appearances of Jesus. The four Gospels and St. Paul (1 Cor 15:3–8) represent different traditions that vary significantly in point of detail, even within the same Gospel, and in spite of perfunctory attempts at synchronization.

perhaps Peter is not at all seeking to deepen his experience of Easter but, on the contrary, trying to forget it. Was it all just a beautiful dream? Moreover, it cannot have helped that the seven disciples labored all night and caught nothing. That sounds ominously like "the real world."

Then, just as day broke, there is a figure on the beach; a greeting. The disciple whom Jesus loved exclaims, "It is the Lord!" When Peter heard that it was the Lord, he put on clothes, for he was naked. Is there a reminiscence here of the Book of Genesis? "Who told you that you were naked? What is this that you have done?" Peter knows well what he has done. He has already wept bitterly about it (Luke 22:62).

Then there is the miraculous draft of fishes—153 of them: from a famine to a feast. Then the invitation, "Come and break your fast." We have bread, and also fish—one of the most ancient symbols for Christ himself. He took the bread and the fish and gave them to the disciples. None of them dared to ask him, "Who are you?" because they knew he was the Lord.

The reconciliation follows. "Simon son of John, do you love me more than these?" "Yes, Lord; you know that I love you." Three times, the same question, three times, the same answer. Peter is wounded that Jesus needs to ask the same question three times. He answers with all his heart the third time, "Lord, you know everything; you know that I love you!" (John 21:10–20). Peter had denied Jesus three times. Jesus gives him the opportunity three times to unsay his denials. Three is the Hebrew superlative.

Three denials mean that Peter really and truly denied

Jesus. Three days in the tomb says that Jesus was really and truly dead, and *four* days says that Lazarus was actually stinking (John 11:39). Three proclamations that the Lord is holy mean that there is none holier. It has survived from the Old Testament, right through to the contemporary Latin liturgy of the Mass. And the acceptance by Jesus of Peter's three protestations of his love tells us that Jesus has really and truly forgiven him for his triple denial.

But there is more. At the Last Supper, in the context of the Eucharist, Jesus had told Peter, "Where I am going, you cannot follow me now; but you will follow afterward." Peter is indignant. "Lord, why can I not follow you now? I will lay down my life for you." It is to be noted that Peter took the perceived snub very personally. There is no mention of the other disciples in his protest. Jesus presents him with the brutal truth. "Will you lay down your life for me? Very truly, I tell you, before the cock crows, you will have denied me three times" (John 13:36–38).

Now, in the aftermath of Peter's triple denial of Jesus, and of his threefold protestation of love, which Jesus counterpoints with the thrice repeated commission to feed his lambs and sheep, Jesus foretells the kind of death by which Peter will glorify God. After this he said to him, "Follow me." And this time, Peter turned and saw the disciple whom Jesus loved following them; he was the one who had reclined next to Jesus at the supper and had said, "Lord, who is it that is going to betray you?" He was also the only disciple to stand with Mary at the foot of the cross. When Peter saw him, he said to Jesus, "Lord, what about him?" He is surely saying, "Lord, this is the disciple whom you love, and he is more worthy of your love than I am." But Jesus answered, "If it is my will that he remain until I come, what is that to you? Follow me!" (John 21).

FOR REFLECTION

1. What is the meaning of the Scripture text at the opening of this chapter, taken from Romans 6:4 and used in the Mass of the Easter Vigil?
2. Does "newness of life" refer to this present life or to some future existence?
3. Who do you say that Jesus is?
4. Does Jesus know that you love him?
5. Has Jesus asked you to follow him?

Chapter 7
EASTER SUNDAY

*When Christ who is your life is revealed, then you will
be revealed with him in glory.* (Col 3:4)

St. Augustine says, "We are an Easter people, and Alleluia is
our song." He means that, even now, though life can still be
very dark, we are in some sense already risen with Christ.
The church is not a "Hallelujah Gang" on a perpetual high.
There are still plenty of hard realities that need to be faced,
but we live in sure hope. If we still have to pray, "Thy kingdom come," and we are not there yet, we remember that
Jesus also said, "The Kingdom of God is within [among]
you" (Luke 17:21). Christ is truly risen. The victory has
been won. This was the essential kerygma of the Gospels and
of the early Church. Paul tells us virtually nothing else that
Jesus did or said. The Easter events, for him, are the heart of
the matter. He says this in many different ways.

St. Peter has the same central idea in his First Epistle.

Blessed be the God and Father of our Lord Jesus Christ! By his great mercy he has given us a new birth into a living hope through the resurrection of Jesus Christ from the dead, and into an inheritance that is imperishable, undefiled, and unfading, kept in heaven for you. (1 Pet 1:3–5)

Jesus risen from the dead is the focus of our faith and hope, and of a joy "so glorious that it cannot be described" (1 Pet 1:8, NJB) These are meant to be the very characteristics by which people recognize us as Christian: "Always be ready to make your defense to anyone who demands from you an accounting for the hope that is in you" (1 Pet 3:15). Faith, hope, mutual love, and joy are to be the signs by which people will know who we are.

In the Creed we say: *et exspecto resurrectionem*. These are indeed great expectations. We have become used to settling for low expectations: money, power, influence, fame, comfort, and a tediously long life, but there is nothing in all that to fill a human heart. Hilaire Belloc observes that whereas kings live in palaces and pigs live in sties, youth lives in expectation—and he adds—that youth is wise.[5]

Let us not rob young people of their dreams, of their birthright, by emphasizing ambition and success too much. We must relearn, and teach how to travel hopefully.

Of course, hope is dangerous. Hope threatens the precarious security of the present moment, the gratification of bread and circuses now. Hope is inseparable from growth,

---

5. Hilaire Belloc, *Complete Verse of Hilaire Belloc* (London: Duckworth, 1970).

change, and creative insecurity. Hope is for those who travel light, for risk takers, and pilgrims. Our culture craves absolute security *now*. This is our Achilles' heel. The terrorists have understood that aspect of our culture.

Let us return again to somebody whom we have mentioned so often in these pages: Peter, the one who had so much difficulty accepting the real Christ that he ended up denying three times that he even knew him—which wasn't quite a lie. We could even say that he did not know the *real* Christ at all. Finally, he was able to hear and act on the summons, "Follow me!"

It takes us sometimes a whole lifetime to learn how to act on this summons in our life. That will be the victory of the Easter Christ in each of us.

FOR REFLECTION

1. From the second reading on Easter Sunday that is quoted at the opening of this chapter, do you believe that Christ really is your life?
2. What does *glory* in the same quotation mean?
3. Do you know who you really are?
4. Who does the person I become depend on: God, myself, or somebody else?

Chapter 8
SEEING AND BELIEVING

"Blessed are those who have not seen and yet have come to believe." (John 20:29)

There are surprising things about the appearances of Jesus after his resurrection. First, he manifests himself and then vanishes again. We might wonder where he was between times. He does say to Mary Magdalene, "I have not yet ascended to the Father." And he commissions her to announce to his brothers, "I am ascending to my Father and your Father, to my God and your God" (John 20:17). So, in the meantime, where is he? Is he possibly spending quality time with his mother, who had seen little of him for the last three years of his public ministry, and whose soul had been indeed pierced with a sword, as foretold by Simeon in the Temple (Luke 2:35). That would be most appropriate. Simply, we do not know.

The second strange thing is a consequence of the first. It is that Jesus, who was constantly in the company of his disciples during the three years of his public life, now seems to have become both elusive and reticent. He visits the disciples to strengthen their faith and to give them courage for the long haul, which is still going on two thousand years later. As Jesus himself said, "It is to your advantage that I go away, for if I do not go away, the Advocate will not come to you; but if I go, I will send him to you" (John 16:7). For better or worse, *we* are now entrusted with the Word of God. But we are not alone. "We are witnesses to these things, and so is the Holy Spirit whom God has given to those who obey him" (Acts 5:32).

On the other hand, when Jesus does appear, it is for real. We are not dealing with a ghost, with some shadowy wisp of smoke on the wall. He does walk in through locked doors—at least twice—but he is no vapory spirit. He allows Thomas and the other disciples to examine his hands and his feet and his side, to even put their fingers and their hands into the wounds that the nails and the lance made in his flesh. He also eats food before their eyes—on at least three occasions.

The most mysterious thing of all is that the disciples do not recognize Jesus until he first says something or does something significant. St. Luke simply says, "Something prevented them from recognizing him." What? Luke does not say. Mary Magdalene thinks that Jesus, whom she knew well, is the gardener!—until he says her name, "Mary." The two disciples at Emmaus, whose hearts are burning within them, do not recognize Jesus until he breaks bread with them; and in the Gospel scene where Peter and six disciples go fishing, it is only when Jesus speaks and acts that the disciple whom he loved says to Peter, "It is the Lord!" Later in that same incident, the evangelist says, "None of the disciples dared to ask him, 'Who are you?' because they knew it was the Lord" (John 21:12).

Perhaps the most curious thing of all, from our modern point of view, is that Jesus never showed himself to Pontius Pilate, who condemned him to death; and he never showed himself to Herod, who treated him like a fool; and he never showed himself to the chief priests and the mob, who clamored and howled for his death, and he never showed himself to the Romans, who crucified him, and even shared out between themselves the clothes on his back. The noble exception is the Roman centurion, who praised God (Luke 23:47), and standing facing Jesus, seeing how he breathed his last, exclaimed, "Truly this man was God's Son!" (Mark 15:39). He never shows himself to Professor Dawkins or to Professor Hitchens, skeptics who need to be convinced.

The reality is that Jesus does not want to triumph over anyone or to prove them wrong. He wants to convert the hearts—even of those who have been his enemies. Jesus said once, attributing his words to Abraham in one of his parables, "If they do not listen to Moses and the prophets, neither will they be convinced even if someone rises from the dead" (Luke 16:31). Mere physical vision is not enough, neither is scientific experimental proof. It may be enough to bring cold intellectual conviction. It can never be enough to give faith, to give hope, to give love. Physical sight can never be enough to convert a single human heart; only Jesus can do that. It is only when he calls our name; it is only when he breaks bread with us, that we can really recognize him.

Jesus said to Thomas, "Have you believed because you have seen me? Blessed are those who have not seen and yet have come to believe" (John 20:29). He was talking about us; he was talking about you; he was talking about me.

"I believe; help my unbelief" (Mark 9:24).

FOR REFLECTION

1. Where do you think Jesus was between his resurrection and ascension?

2. Peter and the Apostles answered the high priest and his council: "We are witnesses to these things, and so is the Holy Spirit whom God has given to those who obey him" (Acts 5:32). As witnesses, have we been doing a good job?

CHAPTER 9

A BENEDICTINE EASTER[6]

*"You have pain now, but I will see you again, and your
hearts will rejoice, and no one will take your joy from
you."* (John 16:22)

Benedictines do have a characteristic "take" on Easter. This
is not so much because Benedictines *enjoy* liturgy, or even
because some of them are liturgists. It is because St. Benedict
himself, in his Rule, puts the Easter experience at the heart
of his understanding of the Christian life.

Benedict was born about AD 480 at Nursia, northeast of
Rome, and died at Monte Cassino in about AD 547. He
never strayed more than a few days journey from the place
of his birth. He was moderately well educated up to the age
of sixteen or seventeen, when he fled, *scienter indoctus* (wisely
unlearned) from the worldly or worse atmosphere of stu-
dent life in Rome. Settling in a cave in the hill country of

---

6. This chapter is an abridged version of the author's article in the *American
Benedictine Review*, December 2003.

Subiaco, he lived as a hermit until early manhood. Then, coaxed from his solitude by some neighboring monks, who thought he might make a good abbot, he eventually founded twelve monasteries.

If two attempts on his life are anything to go by, Benedict was hardly a great abbot at that time. Too ardent perhaps, too idealistic; he was certainly inexperienced and probably intolerant. His famous *Rule for Monks*, written some forty years later at Monte Cassino, bears all the signs of holy wisdom, gentle patience, and a loving understanding of human nature, acquired the hard way, by experience, through many trials, and with not a few mistakes along the way.

Virtually everything we know about Benedict is contained in that Rule or in the charming life of the saint written, most scholars agree, by Pope St. Gregory the Great fifty years after Benedict's death in 547.

There are no spectacular achievements recorded in either document, unless it be some nicely appropriate miracles, which historians would probably discount, or that least dramatic of miracles, which they might not even notice: tiny communities of stable, harmonious, orderly, hospitable, and God-centered life sprouting amidst the rubble of a ransacked and ruined empire.

If men and women today are still turning to communities where *peace, work and pray*, and *prefer nothing to Christ*, are the familiar watchwords, it is surely not in search of sophisticated ideas or esoteric wisdom. They are attracted by a simple art of spiritual living and by the slow-release miracle of God's fidelity and love in the long endurance of daily life.

Taking a lead from Charles Dickens's *A Christmas Carol*, let us talk about Easter past, Easter yet to come, and Easter now.

EASTER PAST

St. Gregory tells the story of young Benedict's Easter:

There was a priest who dwelt far away from the place [where Benedict was] who had prepared a meal for the Easter festivities. The Lord appeared to him in a vision and said, "you are preparing delicacies for yourself, and my servant in such-and-such a place is suffering from hunger." So the priest got up immediately, and at the height of the Paschal celebrations made his way to the place with the food he had prepared. He searched for the man of God among the mountain tops and throughout the valley ravines and in the caves in the ground, and he found him hidden in his grotto.

When they had prayed, they blessed the All-powerful Lord and sat down together. After some pleasant conversation about life, the priest who had come said, "Get up. Let us take some food. For today is Easter." The man of God replied, "I know that it is Easter because I have the honour of seeing you." Far from men, he had overlooked that that day was the solemnity of Easter. The venerable priest insisted, "Seriously, today is the Resurrection of the Lord, Easter day. Cease your abstaining. It is not fitting on this feast. That is why I have been sent to you, so that we may eat together the good things of the All-powerful Lord." They blessed God and had their meal. When the meal was over and they had finished talking, the priest returned to his church.[7]

The biographer adds that some shepherds who came upon Benedict around the same time, "seeing him there among the wild bushes, clothed in skins, took him for an animal." He certainly cannot have looked much like a fledgling churchman.

For a Christian, not knowing when it is Easter must be the nadir of disengagement from sacramental and liturgical practice. Surprisingly, to our way of thinking, this aspect of his story does not seem to bother Pope St. Gregory. Where a modern hagiographer might have a priest bring the teenage hermit communion or even say Mass for him on Easter Sunday, Gregory is content with "delicacies" and "pleasant conversation about life," intermingled, it is true, with some prayers and blessings.

Benedict's regular supplier, Romanus, seems equally unconcerned about sacramental piety and ecclesial affiliation. He provides the youth clandestinely with "the habit of the holy life" and with basic rations, and with nothing else worth mentioning. The situation as presented in Gregory's *Dialogues* is that during all this period—three years by the time of that Easter—Benedict had had little to no access to the sacraments or, very possibly, access to much of the written Scriptures.

This a-liturgical Benedict might appeal to the spiritual cave dwellers of our own day; those who, though they "truly

---

7. St. Gregory the Great, *Dialogues II*, trans H. Costello and E. de Bhaldraithe, commentary by A. de Vogüé (Petersham, MA: St. Bede's 1993), 1:6–7.

seek God" (*Rule of Benedict* 58), do it elsewhere and everywhere except in their own local churches. Skeptical, or at least not attracted by *organized* religion, they do not look to pastors or congregations for help in working out a personal spirituality. For all such, Benedict, the cave dweller, could indeed be patron and paradigm. Although, in later years, he discouraged others tempted to emulate his premature enthusiasm for eremitical living (*RB* 1:3–5), it is precisely in the inchoateness and eccentricity of his youthful ardor that many young people today might find him attractive and strangely contemporary.

Few nowadays will want to live physically in caves but many already do mentally, morally, and spiritually. Seemingly impervious to, or even repelled by the preaching and practice of the churches, which are often perceived through the skewed images of a shallow culture, such people, like Benedict in mid-adolescence, or even like Christ himself on the threshold of his ministry, may be driven by the Spirit "into the wilderness" for a period of struggle and discernment (Mark 1:12)

Those driven by the Spirit *need* more than safe conformity, more than docile routine, whether in synagogue, parish, monastery, or cave. This is the real drama of empty churches today: not the defection to Mammon or to obsessive triviality of the spiritually moribund, but the disengagement of the spiritually alive, of many who do seek and are *driven* to seek, not just a regimen of spiritual exercises, but a spiritual art of living. For such as these, the cave, both physically and metaphorically, may be a necessary initiation to that spiritual art. It is there that one learns "to return to oneself," and "to dwell with oneself." These are expressions used by St. Gregory the Great to describe what Benedict's life in the cave was about.

There is a growing awareness within the Church that some of our gravest problems have sprung from insensitivity, callousness, and even usurpation in respect to the spiritual and emotional integrity of persons still seeking themselves and the truth of their own lives. The most shocking examples of this have been the episodes of sexual abuse of children and adolescents. But the sheer sordidness of those cases should not obscure from us the underlying and more generalized problem: the misuse of power within the institutional Church in areas that impinge upon the dignity and integrity of individual persons. Surely, nothing could be more calculated to drive young people out of the Church and into their caves.

A certain freedom is essential to those *driven* by the Spirit, as it was in Benedict's liturgically impoverished spirituality of the cave. Was it not he who, hearing that Martin the Hermit had chained himself to a rock in his cave, sent an urgent message that the love of Christ alone should bind us rather than chains of iron?

Materially and literally, Benedict's cave was probably a bad idea. His own mature teaching seems to say so. Yet, even if in later years he recalled that *Easter past* with more caution than enthusiasm, he may also have retained some affection for that young hermit who was seeking God so earnestly, as well as gratitude to the good priest who took such trouble finding him.

EASTER YET TO COME

It is true that the life of a monk should always have a Lenten character, but since few have the strength for this, we urge that all alike should keep their life most pure during these days of Lent and wash away in this holy season the negligence of other times. This can be worthily done if we refrain from all evil behavior and devote ourselves to prayer with tears, to reading and compunction of heart, and to the work of abstinence. In these days, therefore, let us add to the usual measure of our service something by way of personal prayer and abstinence from food and drink, so that each can offer to God, of his own will, something above the measure laid down for him, in the joy of the Holy Spirit. In other words, let each one deny his body some food, drink, loose talk and joking, and look forward to holy Easter with the joy of spiritual longing (*RB* 49:1–7).

This chapter on Lent, composed as many as forty years after that Easter spent in a cave, reflects a marked development in Benedict's spirituality. It is not just that the individual caveman has since been absorbed into a community: this whole community is now envisioned together in the space-time dimension of Easter.

We know from the practicalities of the Rule that Easter had become, in Benedict's mind, the pivot for the entire calendar and timetable of work, reading, and feeding programs of the monastery. This chapter on Lent, so markedly influenced by the liturgical sermons of Pope St. Leo the Great, identifies more explicitly than any other the Easter faith-vision suffusing all these material arrangements and activities. The paschal mystery has become for Benedict what it should be in any mature Christian spirituality: the heart and focus of faith, hope, and love.

When Benedict writes, in what is clearly the summation phrase of the whole chapter, that we should "look forward to holy Easter with the joy of spiritual longing," he is not thinking primarily about Easter 539 or 540. He is defining what he understands the whole of monastic life, and indeed of Christian life, to be about. He is explaining what he means by saying that the life of a monk should always have a Lenten character.

Benedict is not advocating a very penitential regime, one so full of mortifications and self-denial that few would have the strength for it. On the contrary, one has the impression that the penitential element is a corrective required during Lent, only because we habitually fall short of something more fundamental at other times. When he goes on to give examples of the privations he has in mind, there is nothing very terrifying about them: "To refrain from all evil behavior." He could not decently ask for less than that. For the rest, he is content to urge each one to choose *something* that he can do *freely* and *joyfully*. The examples suggested amount to little more than what most sensible people routinely undertake nowadays to preserve psychological balance, good health, and a pleasant appearance—even if Benedict's motivation was certainly more God-centered.

The penitential element in the "Lenten life" is a preliminary —a corrective that has to do with freeing oneself for something more important; something that should be central all year round. The real issue about freedom is not what we need to free ourselves *from* but rather what we want to be free *for*. Without some worthwhile objective, freedom is merely a burden. In Sartre's phrase, *on est condamné à être libre*. As dictators everywhere have understood, people in general are not very interested in freedom. According to such an acute observer as the Emperor Nero, all they really want is *bread and circuses*. He might say nowadays, *beer and ball games*.

Benedict *is* interested in freedom. His "Lenten life" cuts back on bread and circuses so that, at least for forty days, we can be free to do what we should be doing all the time and every day: looking forward to holy Easter with the joy of spiritual longing: *Pascha expectet*. This *expectation* is no mere annual ritual; it is the heart of Christian faith. *Et exspecto resurrectionem*, as we proclaim in the Creed, is the strong focus of the monk's unwavering hope. "I shall live," he proclaims on the day of his profession, "and you will not disappoint me in my great expectations" (*RB* 58:21). Benedict bids the monk "to yearn for eternal life with all spiritual longing" (*RB* 4:46). This phrase is unmistakably parallel with the key expression in the chapter on Lent, "to look forward to holy Easter with the joy of spiritual longing" (*RB* 49:7b). The monk's longing for Easter is not seasonal. It is perennial.

Expectation, longing, hope: three words epitomizing the inner dynamic of Christian life. Therefore, it is not surprising that Benedict summarizes the entire resources of the monastic "workshop" in the maxim: "Never lose hope in God's mercy" (*RB* 4:74).

Hope is not proactive, which is a difficulty for a society where people are valued and value themselves in terms of achievement: "What you see is what you get, and what you get is what I am worth." With hope, as opposed to ambition, the center of gravity is elsewhere, and one must wait. Yet hope is not passive, it is not hand-folding resignation. Hope is profoundly dynamic, motivating, and empowering. This conviction lies at the heart of the Easter kerygma.

EASTER NOW

The victory of Easter is both yet to come and already with us now. "We are an Easter People," St. Augustine proclaims, "and Alleluia is our song." The monastic liturgy as described in the *Rule of Benedict* uses "*Alleluia*," not just in the Easter season, like the Great Church, but throughout the year except during Lent. Our *Easter Now* of every day is inseparably linked to that great *Easter yet to come*. "Alleluia is our song." This does not mean a life of facile celebration.

Benedict never loses sight of the Easter mystery in its totality—cross and resurrection. We "persevere in the Lord's teaching in the monastery until death, sharing through patience in the sufferings of Christ, that we may also deserve to share in his kingdom" (*RB* Prol 50).

Cassian, one of the Fathers of monasticism, says in one of his profoundest insights:

Our cross is the fear of the Lord. Just as someone who has been crucified can no longer move or turn his limbs this way or that, so neither can we act out our desires and yearnings in accordance with what is easy and gives us pleasure at the moment, but in accordance with the law of the Lord and where it constrains us.[8]

In this sense, we must indeed take up our cross daily and follow Christ. The weight of that cross is not just the bad things that happen: it is especially the routine daily patience, as well as the sometimes more costly fortitude required to adhere to God's will and cling to the reality of our own lives. "He holds fast to patience with a quiet mind, enduring, not weakening or running away" (*RB* 7:35–36).

In speaking of the *reality of our lives*, we turn to that quest for "purity of heart," which Cassian mentions, directly or equivalently, more than two hundred times in his writings. Purity of heart implies integrity, limpidity, freedom from self-deception and from the tyranny of anger, lust, self-pitying sadness, discouragement, and all those other "demons" whose evil work is to lead us away from reality and into a world of selfish preoccupation, pointless misery, and anxiety.

The Greek word *katharos*, which we translate as "pure" in the expression, "a pure heart," actually means "purified." It implies the ongoing work of grace and of our own unrelenting struggle for integration.[9] It is this work that Benedict enjoins upon his monks during Lent and throughout life

---

8. John Cassian, *The Institutes*, trans. Boniface Ramsey (New York: Newman Press, 2000), 4:35.

9. Columba Stewart, *Introduction to Purity of Heart in Early Ascetic and Monastic Literature*, ed. H. Luckman and L. Kulzer (Collegeville, MN: The Liturgical Press, 1999).

(*RB* 49:2). It is a way of the cross, but one bathed already in the light of Easter.

As the transforming power of Christ's paschal mystery works within us, our life is inseparably Lent and Easter, purification and paradise, death and resurrection.

FOR REFLECTION

1. Is there much difference between the young Benedict and a teenager of our own day? What spiritual values do they have in common?
2. Is Nero, the Roman Emperor, right—that most people are not interested in freedom?
3. What do you want to be free from?
4. What do you want to be free for?

Chapter 10

REMEMBERING HIS WORDS

> *"Remember how he told you, while he was still in Galilee, that the Son of Man must be handed over to sinners, and be crucified, and on the third day rise again." Then they remembered his words.* (Luke 24:6–8)

We need to remember the words of the Lord Jesus. They are for us light and hope, especially in times of darkness and sadness. So, yes, let us remember the words of our Savior.

> "I am the resurrection and the life. Those who believe in me, even though they die, will live, and everyone who lives and believes in me will never die." (John 11:25–26)

> "Do not let your hearts be troubled. Believe in God, believe also in me…If it were not so, would I have told you that I go to prepare a place for you? And if I go

and prepare a place for you, I will come again and will take you to myself, so that where I am, there you may also be." (John 14:1–3)

"You have pain now; but I will see you again, and your hearts will rejoice, and no one will take your joy from you." (John 16:22)

"Father…you have sent me and have loved them even as you have loved me. Father, I desire that those also, whom you have given me, may be with me where I am, to see my glory, which you have given me because you loved me before the foundation of the world." (John 17:21–24)

"Truly I tell you, today you will be with me in paradise." (Luke 23:43)

These are the words of the Lord. Their meaning is clear and unmistakable. Founded on the paschal mystery, on the death and resurrection of Christ that we commemorate and celebrate in each Mass, these words bring us to the heart of our Christian faith and hope.

So what *do* we hope for? St. Paul exclaims:

If for this life only we have hoped in Christ, we are of all people most to be pitied. But in fact Christ has been raised from the dead, the first fruits of those who have died (1 Cor 15:19–20).

It is Paul, too, who wrote:

I am convinced that neither death, nor life, nor angels, nor rulers, nor things present, nor things to come, nor powers, nor height, nor depth, nor anything else in all creation will be able to separate us from the love of God in Christ Jesus our Lord (Rom 8:38–39).

Dying he destroyed our death.
Rising he restored our life.
Lord Jesus, come again in glory.

FOR REFLECTION

1. Read and reflect on the words of Jesus about death.
2. St. Francis famously referred to "Sister Death." Can we be comfortable with the thought of death?